AF752416

retrovirology

pitt poetry series

Nancy Krygowski and Jeffrey McDaniel, *Editors*

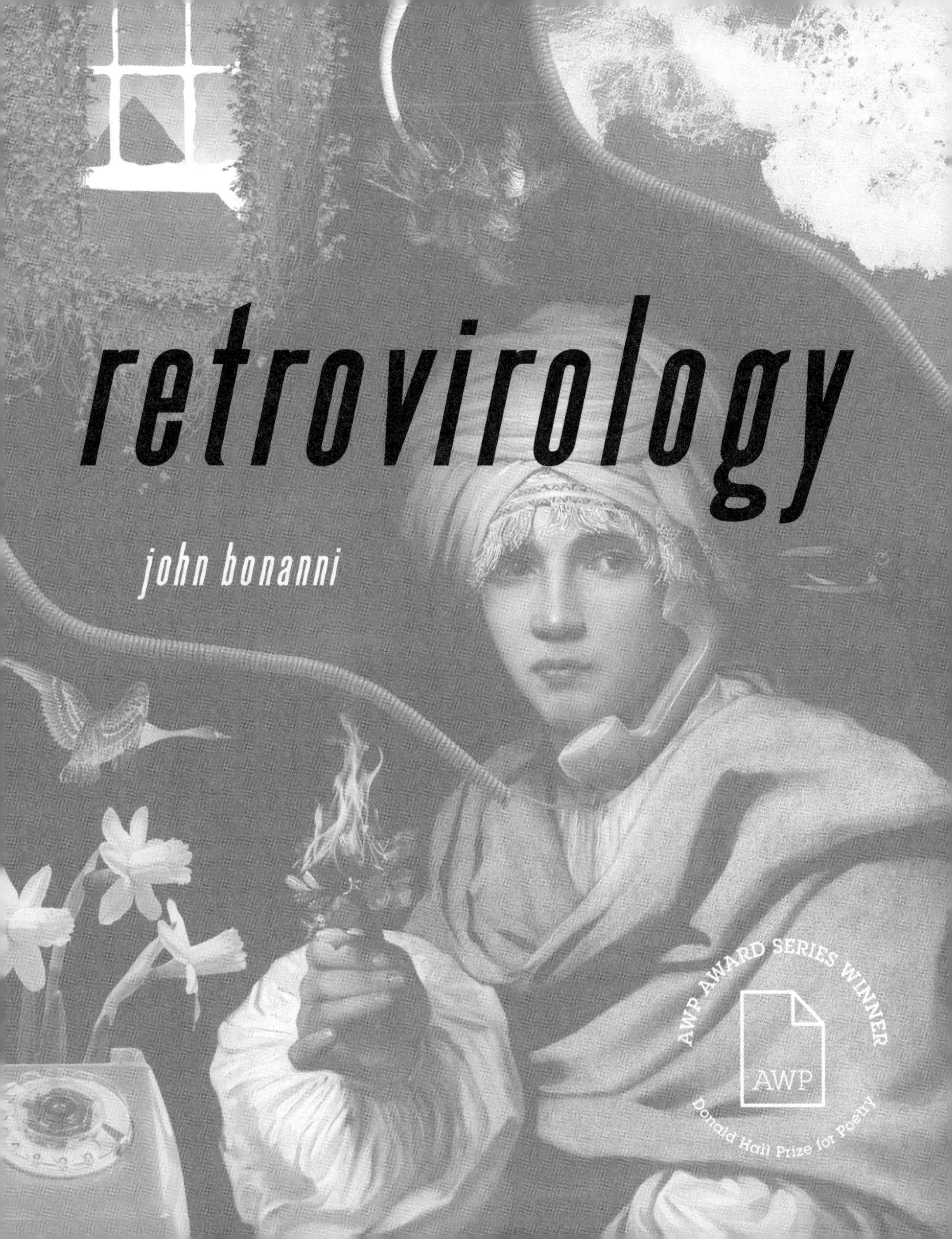
retrovirology
john bonanni
AWP AWARD SERIES WINNER
AWP
Donald Hall Prize for Poetry

This book is the winner of the 2025 Donald Hall Prize for Poetry, awarded by the Association of Writers and Writing Programs (AWP), and selected by Honorée Fanonne Jeffers. AWP, a national organization serving more than three hundred colleges and universities, has its headquarters at George Mason University, Mail Stop 1E3, Fairfax, VA 22030.

The Donald Hall Prize for Poetry is made possible by the generous support of Amazon.com.

Published by the University of Pittsburgh Press, Pittsburgh, Pa., 15260
Copyright © 2026, John Bonanni
All rights reserved
Manufactured in the United States of America
Printed on acid-free paper
10 9 8 7 6 5 4 3 2 1

ISBN 13: 978-0-8229-6835-1
ISBN 10: 0-8229-6835-5

Cover art by Alex Wolfe, using Michael Sweerts, *Boy in a Turban Holding a Nosegay,* oil on canvas, 76.4 x 61.8 cm, Museo Nacional Thyssen-Bornemisza, Madrid, and some elements via Adobe Stock.

Book design by Alex Wolfe

Publisher: University of Pittsburgh Press, 7500 Thomas Blvd., 4th floor, Pittsburgh, PA 15260, United States, www.upittpress.org

EU Authorized Representative: Easy Access System Europe, Mustamäe tee 50, 10621 Tallinn, Estonia, gpsr.requests@easproject.com

for the elders

and for Maria

contents

Sonnet for Every Man Who Died When I Was Born 3

i. elegy

Rare Cancer 7

First Kiss 8

Reverse Abecedarian with Mostly Missing Vowels 10

Billboard of an empty bed 11

Will 13

35-Year-Old Man Shares Joint Near Harbor of Gay Resort Town 15

Elegy for Gaëton Dugas 17

Installation: Anita Bryant 20

Methodology 21

Lung Study 22

Elegy for Larry Kramer 23

Collective 27

Window 29

ii. the coat room was the first to go

Death of the Sperm Whale 33

Neighbors 34

I, Barbie 37

Godspell 39

Boy in a Turban Holding a Nosegay 41

Abecedarian with Missing Vowels 43

Wind in the Air, Wind in the Lungs 44

The rain gutter deserves a better cleaning 46

Drug Buddy 48

Abecedarian in a Gay Porn 50

Inventing Safe Sex: Questions from Richard Berkowitz & Michael Callen 51

Beautiful People 53

Rubin 55

iii. we stuck our hard dicks in

Reverse Abecedarian with Missing Vowels 59

Notes for a concrete poem 60

Jericho 61

Rag Protest, 1985 62

Pyramid 63

Wellcome 64

Wellcome Detail 70

Wall Street 72

Coalescence 74

Bowers vs. Hardwick 77

iv. mirror for mirror

Stoke 81

Variations on a Theme in Blue 82

A Rose for Simon 84

Abecedarians with Consonants Who Have Left First the Party and Then Their Bodies 86

Command 88

Memorial 89

Parallel Trial 91

Last Supper 92

On Saving the Old Bouquet 95

Notes 97

Acknowledgments 101

retrovirology

Sonnet for Every Man Who Died When I Was Born

Touch the face, though you don't know it.
Stroke stubble of a beard still growing
beneath your palm. Touch this face, cold
as it is. Leave pennies on the eyelids.
Touch the face though you don't know it, it
knows you. It doesn't feel real, does it? Touch it
anyway. Touch this face, each embalmed skin
cell frosting through. Let the island of your hand
fall cold with this touch. Let your cuticles ice
over, your fingernails, the deepest shade of blue.
Hold your touch there, longer. Hold it down
until he turns to ash. Then, with newly stained
fingers, anoint yourself. A figure eight across
your forehead. He is the one who saved you.

i. elegy

How thin the distance made you
—Thom Gunn

Rare Cancer

In the period October 1980 to May 1981, five young men, all active
one of the investigators, described the appearance of the outbreak
as "rather devastating" Patient 1: A previously healthy
33-year-old man *have been diagnosing the condition*
among younger men two-month history of fever *all of whom said*
The patient's condition deteriorated despite courses
of treatment with *that they were homosexual*
Patient 2: A previously healthy 30-year-old man
most cases had involved homosexual men
who have had multiple April 1981 after a five-month history
of fever each day *as many as 10 sexual encounters*
each night up to four times a week but, as of the latest reports,
he continues to have a fever each day
Many of the patients also reported that they had used drugs
Patient 3: A 30-year-old man was well until *Dr. Curran said*
that there was no apparent danger to non-homosexuals from contagion
Patient 4: A 29-year-old man developed
serious malfunctions did not improve after being
given intravenous *in two types of cells*
and died in March *called T and B cell lymphocytes*
Patient 5: A previously healthy 36-year-old man
the researchers did not know whether The diagnosis
was confirmed for all five patients *the immunological defects*
were the underlying problem reported having frequent homosexual
contacts with various *or drug use* reported using
inhalant *is testing various hypotheses*

First Kiss

The school bus tenses and rumbles &,
(this is where the heterosexual inserts
themself into the poem) today, it neither hurts

nor pleases. Eros takes a seat in the back
of the bus, ripped pleather pasted green
with the scent of fixative, unnatural. He sits

between her plaid skirt & my tightening thigh.
The engine groans with fury, my bony ass moving
back & forth like a character in a movie I had seen

once or maybe every day of my life. Someone out-
side my body invites her there, opening her soft lips
& braces. Her name: Jess. When he tongues

her desperate mouth, he begins to disappear.
The window, open just a crack so that first
he's stealth, moving into my chest then out

of my chapped lips & onto the latch. Tongues
braid like wet snakes breeding in swamps.
I pull away. Turn, unvirgined. See? See my man-

hood walking down this shaking aisle to a place
on the bus where privacy acts panicked? See
how it roams free like an altared son, or a bow

or sports? He's out that window, banging
against the yellow fender's body, dumped
to the street like some used apple core. He's

gone, but still hissing—may I say it?—loudly.

Reverse Abecedarian with Mostly Missing Vowels

Zapped the skin like an electrode during
your shock treatment then stared at two
X's covering the eye lids—what causes it?
Who did the damage in what year? When
vespers sung crawled across the twilit sky into
taut clouds to cover these constellated gods,
stretched & striating their muscles of light, they all
reform into a disregarded ceiling hovering over
Queer Boy Scout campfires while an ember
pulled from the timber reaches for another
notch in the lubricated rope.
My, how it whispers, the heart
left to itself to calm the fuck down.
Kleenex moist now hardening into stain
jostled & crumpled into this portrait:
Him. Skin, imagined & retrained, as even
Glaucus plucks the salt sea grass & chews
for the crunch of it. How's that taste?
Dive in & become it, wave foam & crest,
catcalling Ganymede back from the night,
breakers from Troy, as though the only way to steal
away is by drowning.

Billboard of an empty bed

after Félix González-Torres

sunlight on the ruffled sheets
cave of a whitened excavation
pillow top, used, thread count loose
who rose
from the king size depression
who too tired
to fix these sheets
who you & you
two head crowns
displaced from rest
overtake of overpass
to look up to an empty
bed of billboard
fossil of a body
sure we call the sheets
white but the light
hits harder at certain edges
the rest
slips to gray
such shadows
crest these waves
behind the pillows
a negation
beneath them
a shadow
now moonlight on the sun-
light on the ruffled sheets

whose were you
sheets unrested or
sheets for shroud
down comfort
rising up
for a moment
we could enter it
if only we could lie
while standing

Will

willed you back but only part
of you came   will

not forget the fire you built
for me on a cold september

night your furnace so heavy
& breathing   willed it on back

only some will float through   ash
as though the graveyard

that lifts me up cannot
fully sustain me either

willed you forth so I could
shake your hand   lip

the words thank you   & say again
kiss your forehead your lips

say again wash   your feet so say
your will be done your will

inherited despite the probate   will
from william from *wil* as in desire

& *helm* as helmet meaning   protection
I stitch a black backpack around

your whole will stitch straps
to the back   slide it through

my shoulders left then right
will fasten again will return

so say again will
you come back

35-Year-Old Man Shares Joint Near Harbor of Gay Resort Town

I bought a six pack & sat down / by Provincetown Harbor. Just off Commercial Street, busy with the ruin / of homosexually gentrified tourism, you can sneak / away, down an alleyway / by Julie Heller Gallery, to a stretch / of beach behind all / the restaurants & retail stores. Here, you can catch / the sunlight with an eerie feeling of privacy / that isn't really at all private. If you plant / yourself somewhere on the sand, you can listen to the waves, / bay side, even, / calm.

// After I finished my first beer, two boys / ambled from behind the alleyway, / & sat down near some drift wood, / about ten feet away from the sandy plot / where I had landed. *What? Him? / He doesn't care.* & because I was a little buzzed, / I said, *Yeah. If anything / I'd take a puff.* I was joking but not really joking. / I hadn't been high in a while / & I did, admittedly, miss that tingly feeling / I got in my face, the feeling of knowing some secret / joke that nobody else knew. *Sure, man. / You want some?*

// The older one was frayed / in every direction. Young, but holding onto / old grit. Someone I would have gained / immense affinity for as a kid / in the nineties. Maybe missing / a tooth or two, but still gorgeous, in that way / that only some sort of / combination of urban wilderness / & youth can make one gorgeous. / He introduced his friend, some 19-year-old whose name / I can't remember. *Still a baby*, / the boy said.

// I took a few puffs because / that's all it takes for me now. I never liked being / high when I was closeted. / It made me paranoid, & because I'm about 135 pounds, I nearly always overdid it, sinking / into a couch, / worrying about identity, never speaking. / I chose to drink instead, picked a substance that would lower / my inhibitions rather than magnify them. / After I came out I understood the draw. / The heightened sensitivity. / The feeling of connectedness in passing / around a joint & feeling the same way.

// The older one kept talking. His / conversation was really one way, / so I didn't have to say much about myself, & I / was thankful for that. / He was a local. He went to Provincetown / High School, which was now closed. / We knew some of the same families. I acted / local even though I lived about 40 minutes away. / *What kind of beer you drinking?*

// I showed it to him.

// *Oh, damn. That shit used to be / like two bucks when they first started. That family, / the Souzas started it outta my boy's / basement. How much did you pay for it?*

// *Eleven.*

// His brow peaked toward the sun. / *Eleven? Shit's a rip off.*

// I felt like a fake momentarily. Posh. / Tourist gay. Gentrified. Remembered / when I drank Pabst Blue Ribbon / because there were no other options, / then thought: I would likely / never see these boys again, / & even if I do, I can ignore them. Being / here was a kind of vacation / for me, where, for them, / here was a place where they were stuck, / straight boys, breeders, feet buried in the harbor.

// High & sensitive, I changed / the subject. *I just checked out that AIDS / memorial in the center of town. Have you / guys seen it?*

// *AIDS is like the new thing,* the fringe boy said. / *Ya know why? Everyone died / & now those people who died, their friends / are dying because now they're old. / And they're all realizing there's gonna be no one left / to say anything.*

// The 19-year old / said, *Didn't some flight / attendant spread it around?*

Elegy for Gaëton Dugas

who *picked up men wherever he went*

who donated his blood

who *I am the prettiest one*

who donated

The Appalling Saga of Patient Zero

whose zero meant O as in letter O as in

Out of California & though

AIDS came to the United States in 1959

& before that, central Africa, about 1930

who did not slaughter a chimpanzee for meat

but who *The Monster Who Gave Us AIDS*

donated his blood to

slides to lab tests to electron microscopes

who *The Columbus of AIDS*

let the tip of the needle draw his blood

for more   a vaccine   a scape   an answer but who

was *a strange guy at the Eighth and Howard bathhouse*

a blonde with a French accent

who said, *Gay cancer. Maybe you'll get it too.*

although who at that time could

not have possibly known

that what he had was transmitted

through sex though a publicist

who, for a book on the subject, stated,

It's the worst kind of yellow journalism

& said, *Don't blame Randy*

who admitted to making it up to compete for sales even

though *Patient Zero: The Man Who Brought AIDS*

to California whose zero now coming

to mean the first

who spread it   despite being the first

who did extend one bone white arm

who made a fist

& who could, at once, at first

see the vein

Installation: Anita Bryant

— Ceiling: Measure dimensions of ceiling.
          — Fit repeated images of album cover
          to ceiling dimensions.

— Walls: Hang from fishing lines
          spheres, painted bright orange.
          —Arrange in rows.

— Bible pages hang down from the center of the ceiling
          & spiral through the center of the room.
          Pauline Letters? Old Testament Scripture? Leviticus.

— Lighting: Position flood lights from the ground.
          — Soft. Ambient.
          — 30 Watt.
          — Accent the corners of the Bible verses.

— Sound: Invite viewer to press Start
          on the record player
          to lower the needle.
          "Paper Roses," the first song on the album, plays.

— Floor: a patchwork, life-size body, male, stitched from my cargo shorts and flannel.

— Title: Save Our Children.

Methodology

— AZT Phase II Trail

☐ Collect 282 People with AIDs (PWAs)

☐ Screen them

☐ All 282 subjects must discontinue
any & all pneumocystis pneumonia medications

☐ None may have Kaposi's Sarcoma

☐ All must agree to live at the hospital grounds in Bethesda, MD

☐ CD4 cell count must be below 500

☐ Give 141 of the subjects
1500 mg capsules by mouth
of AZT

☐ Let 141 people die

☐ Publish study

☐ Add study to C.V.

Lung Study

the fever
build up
lungs
as in
I had
the tape
red
fungal mouth
a vision
opportunistic infection
effective treatment
without
placebo
no script
no placebo
deaths
designed
treatment
or redesign
redesign

the cough
high
of fluid
opportunistic
an opportunity
adhered layered
as cell counts
fungal throat
loss of retinal
KS   prophylaxis as
do not
double   blind
study
without placebo
without their
rising
for death no
without takeover
study
by takeover

Elegy for Larry Kramer

I braced myself for a tornado, and I found a teddy bear.
—Eric Marcus on Larry Kramer

You just knew that he cared more about Yale than he would ever care about you.
—Larry Kramer on Yale University psychiatrist, Dr. Fry

I love being gay.
—Larry Kramer on Larry Kramer

Each quill pen you pull from the ink
colors a tranquil scene
of coconut trees, of palm,
of low tide, & fish scent,
with a portrait of my body in recline,
sand spilled against my thighs,
balls out & shaft tilted right—
until pinion penetrates paper
& you just keep drawing, hard fist
against the desk, jut scratch of woodcut:
Paper in pieces & you alone.

*

The teddy bear you were given
had no eyes & was made of stone.
When they tried to fix this,
the doctors took spoons to your eyes,
a transplant for the bear. That didn't work.
That didn't work at all.

*

In 1953, you gazed into a black room
with a red rose & a red light
& you thought, *What a nice room.*
You thought, *What a nice double mattress.*
then thought it awful
everyone calling it awful
those two men asleep on it.

*

Count each blue pill
one aspirin for each day in the womb
& swallow in handfuls of silence.

*

Stomach push in, stomach pull out, suction
for resuscitation like the pump
in the plumbing they use to flush out
your kitchen sink vomit. Now you live
in New York City & that used to be a pasture.
Before that, another land
mass. Before that, under water.
& maybe the land mass was formed by a volcano.

*

Paper stacks & weighted, a book
against a desk lamp, its title: *Faggots*
with your name across its spine.

*

You see them on the street, kiss their cheeks.
You see them beneath the covers
of blue electric blankets.
You see them on the street, kiss their cheeks.
You see them in the bleached room
at Sloan Kettering.
You see them on the street, kiss their cheeks.
You see them at the bleached room again.
You smell the ash,
You smell the moldy church.
The dust from the hymnal rises.
You see them on the streets but it's not them,
just paling apparitions taking shape.
You pick up a quill pen,

*

write, redraw the teddy bear, & scream,
organize a small brigade
of toy soldiers. You place them
strategically around the board,
red, yellow, blue, a game of Risk.
Then you argue with them—

*

I don't know if a volcano made New York.
Maybe I'm making it all up. I know
some called you a bitch until you died.
Then, in the clear black & white of the paper
there was a large halo placed behind your head.
No, not the hollowed out one. The kind
that looks like a giant yellow pill. That kind
that, against the soft folds of each throat's hard swallow,
catches in the pharynx, then clings there, holding.

Collective

memory died in the mid-nineties with the birth

of cargo shorts & with the halted heartbeats

of hemophiliacs & gay men, some intubated, some alone

in New York apartments, tubes circulating through the venting

& this is *not* an obit: If each tube snakes its way out the window,

then where does memory go? Somewhere into the cold, winter

air, picked up by a breeze, & what is a breeze but a circle?

High temperatures to low, up to down, returning never ending.

A breeze can go anywhere if it catches the right convection current.

Today, one breeze picked the oak leaves up off of the front lawn & I thanked

it because: less raking. Less neighborly judgment. Less & less & less.

The memory is a jagged rock that fell from this breeze, a rock

a person picks up off the lawn, then gives to the next person,

younger, who happens to be a lapidary who then polishes it into a ruby,

& gives it to another person, younger, who likes the ruby, likes its shine,

likes the way it bounces the light, squints in admiration. That person places

it on the window sill until the next person finds it. That person says,

What a nice stone. I wonder what it's for.

Window

like a mouth   you behind a shut window   rose baby's breath sunflower

window   buttercup crocus calla lily   enter   you behind a shut window

daisy gardenia carnation open and close   like a mouth   you behind

a shut window rose baby's breath sunflower   press yourself against the glass

rhododendron, tulip   scratch this glass   shatter it   you behind a shut

you behind a shut window you behind a shut window you behind a shut

[vertical, read bottom to top:]

you behind a shut window   daisy gardenia carnation   open and close

iris daffodil rose peony lily chrysantheum dahlia marigold lavendar lilac

iris daffodil rose peony lily chrysantheum dahlia marigold lavendar lilac

press yourself against the glass pane   you behind a shut window   holly

ii. the coat room was the first to go

My brother will come . . . to ask forgiveness of his father . . . and my father will call me that Sunday night and he will say, Sonia, Sonia, Sonia, it's okay with Wilson and me now. It's okay. We're okay. It's great to have a son.

—Sonia Sanchez

Death of the Sperm Whale

At the Whaling Museum in New Bedford,
my father & I walk into a life-
size ship of what a vessel might
have looked like for the long need
of whale slaughter. Everyone
is here on a Saturday. We walk
around the deck & duck our heads
in the same way any sailor would
& just like a real sailor, you, too, can touch
wood & you, too, can hit your head on the mast.
We roam to a Plexiglas table
to peer into the quarters below:
Small, claustrophobic. A group
of school children climbs aboard.
A chaperone tells them to stay together,
but they don't.
One child disappears
into the laughter.
Another child
won't stop crying.
He is afraid of the stairs.

Neighbors

Delaware County, Pennsylvania, 1994

When the hurricane hits the night club around the corner
          my father calls it an act of God   If we stare
long enough   inside it   we see

          one organ   a robot   that descends
from a disco ball ceiling   One neighbor, Sabine, teaches us
          to break the butts   off lightning bugs   *Who are*

Delilah's Dolls? I ask my brother   *Strippers*   that Pulsations
          hired who ride   up the pole   then down it like
a property value   or wind   With church women my mother

          in heels   barrels up   past the club's glass-sharded
pavement   sign gripped into her pink nail
          polished fingers   *Real Men Don't Need Porn*

My brother   two sisters & I ride Huffies and Schwinns down
          the hill to the McLaughlins   & drink their Kool Aid
Sabine says, *Attach them to your skin*   & we glow

          two bracelets of phosphorescence   that circle
our slim wrists, two rings   of stars   My sister flicks
          a hologram   on her new driver's license   purple light

bent and refracted   into a Pennsylvania stamp   Up the hill
    we leave the McLaughlins   red-lipped
little clowns   When the hurricane hit   my sister's mouth

    open while   Doug McLaughlin's dark hair crests
across his brow   in a small goodbye   Our skin sticks
    to neon clothes   flashing   into the night   warning

signs   for fireflies while we search   for each other to die
    Ghost   Two front yard Japanese maples strain
with wild reach into a lit sky   *Hide there*   Ghost

    in the graveyard   man hunt   Doug's hair
draping across his pool brown eyes   Doug's arms, two maps
    Who wouldn't stare? Searched   for the kill

then trudge   Route 1   find a garden
    center where   we inhale lilies   lavender
mulch & cash in   fizzling   Sprite & a lollipop

    that lasts for days   My sister drives us to Toland Pool
air fits of chlorine   we dive   head first off the high
    into indigo   for such new sex

staring at us from a lifeguard stand   Matt   a gaze like a god's
    When the hurricane hit   it took a dance club's wall
with it   *We prayed*   *Pulsations away,* says my mother

    When the hurricane hit   a god's hold on
our shedding bodies   Next to the garden
    center   a torn-out   Pulsations

its parking lot of popped beer bottles   a pale meadow
    I bike there with Kevin   the building   a fenced-
off skeleton   If we stare long enough   at a disco

    ball ceiling   a robot descends   Now cycle   the lot   & scan
for glass   shards   the broken bottles   scan for all
    that   leftover light

I, Barbie

with a line from Paul Lisicky

i.

"It's all polished and curated and maybe on the way to cold, not a body hair or blemish in sight.

First it was Dylan. No first it was Ken. Plastic
blond Ken with thick chest Ken & curve
of groin, more pouch than dick. A hairless
halo of sex enough to pump through Barbie & me—
Hardened plastic. Studded pouch. Oh Ken. Can you?

ii.

But what else should I expect in the age of AIDS,

& maybe Cody came after. *Baywatch.* Tuft of blond
hair chest bare blue eyed & pink lipped
my eyes gently cradling your half dozen egg abs dive
further down your silk bulge lines of arm
your red rescue can your red suit
your red suit your red suit red
David Chokachi as Cody

iii.

where bodies are getting prematurely old

Then, even still, Dylan:
such white washed glasses to peer into
How best to infantilize our bodies as
young enough to still be hard
How best to fuck him? Or soften
into someone fuckable? Do I just pretend
I am Brenda or Kelly caught in the silk
bed sheets of Beverly Hills? Do I take him in
my own crusty flannel,
an *Entertainment Weekly* tucked
beneath my covers?

iv.

in the houses to the right and left of us?"

Don't tell the neighborhood I play with
Sabine's Barbies don't tell my deep Mattel
secrets—mouth shut, even if your breath heaves
even if my drool leaks
She has Skipper she has the Dream House
She has Ken's shorts we can dress & rip away
She has the car
& it's a pink convertible

Godspell

for Jeffrey Mylett, 1949–1986

Let your throat defer the first verse.
Let your song be sung only on the soundtrack

Let those who are in Judea flee to the mountains
but not the film. Let the director tell you

to start slowly, to save it
Let him who is on the housetop not go down

to take what is in his house to save it
for the end. Let each octave swim:

Stained? We pray for sanctity!
each note swing & ripple—*Love!*

That calls us lovingly.
Let go of them completely:

We beseech thee! Hear us!
Then let the kazoo sound,

the flowers fall to their palms,
let the lilies be placed behind our ears.

Let him who is in the field not turn back to take his mantle.
Let the beep the boom the chick in

for the promised heavenly prize
of your voice to be recognized, but not known?

Let the day's own trouble be sufficient for the day.
Let us not forget unforgettable lungs.

Leave your gift there before the altar and go
& afterward, let your lantern fall

& set the stage ablaze.
The eye is the lamp of the body

So that, after you die, let us all
sing it worse than

you. Let us reach. Let us pray let
you *enter by the narrow gate.*

Boy in a Turban Holding a Nosegay

after Michael Sweerts, Oil on canvas. 76.4 x 61.8 cm
Museo Nacional Thyssen-Bornemisza, Madrid

It's not that his sisters dressed him up, not
that he can't carry,

the large glowing weight on his head,
with its blonde bangs,

small golden threads curling into possibility.
He can, every pound

of the turban, chin up, & facing you.
It's not even the fall

of the blue shawl landing heavily
along the balls

of his shoulders. Even he knows,
this drape will fall

where it will, even a kind of freedom
to it. & even

he'll tell you it's not that the sleeves
of the shirt—

colossal, fabulous puffs of cloud—surround
his delicate wrists—

one suspended, the other hiding his lap—
just below the red sash

knotted around his waist. No, that's not it.
He might tell you

he's tired, & that's partly true. He might
tell you it's allergies,

all the blooming, & that's a lie. There's a comfort
to that sweet smell

of the nosegay held between his burnished fingers,
so much comfort—so

what is it? A pinky hangs in the air,
ready to point.

Abecedarian with Missing Vowels

Broken from the one step onto plate I fake fracture,
coordinate relief not from the whole game, but from knowing I'd be
dead from it. The key in PE is to cough, to stay pale the whole time
flop the right arm around & wince wince *It must be from sliding, that*

glide I took into first base. Who would know from memory?
How? The water fountain always needed in gym class, yet still
jacking from scent of boy sweat & mesh short. Who would
know? Only some small set I never met, never saw—a stone wall between

Lachesis & Clotho, sisters who can't even share their cigarettes, only two tin can
makeshift telephones to echo each raspy, sleep-deprived sentence into each
neck. Their conversation, barely audible, waving through a strung up
phone line cut so that the old canned corn rusts on the floor, now collects

quick & quaking raindrops for some later thirst. It's kickball.
Right foot, laces out, another strike, new player dug out. In right field I
sit down in the grass, picking each dandelion, one stalk at a time,
to loom into a new necklace, knot the green tubes, dot with yellow. U-

VA rays lift their heels, tighten their calves slow dive down into the outfield.
Who would know? Atropos calls me in, takes out a pair of shears that look like an
X, then plunges a blade deep into the ball. *You weren't playing anyway*, she says.
You always show up to ruin everything, I tell her. *You were supposed to be playing*

zones, she snaps, then snips my dandelion necklace, cut & broken little suns.

Wind in the Air, Wind in the Lungs

This time it's a charter flight picking up lag in the current.
Some pilot wears dark

sunglasses. Some goose follows in its wake
thinking the plane its mother. The bird

cranes its neck like a telephone wire
caught in a tree. It honks its sad song

into the air & the high pressure shifts to low
then back to high again causing the rest

of us to wipe the hair from our faces.
I'm small.

This wind: My jeans are grass-stained,
my ass wet.

When we were kids we counted our bruises. Youngest of four,
I always had the most.

The worst one, gray, then shifting to purple & blue along my left thigh.
Dear Charlie horse, it took years before I turned

into a Power Ranger, the yellow one because I was always a better girl,
but not yet pink with a miniskirt.

It was all flips & kicks & slams from there:
I learned the power of my legs,

but only used it in play, came to wish I had used it in the parking lot
of the AMC where I let Rusty

push me to the ground. *Faggot*, he said. My friends, always girls,
yelling *Stop!* I didn't fight back.

His fists, two hammers, drove the breath from just below my pacifist poncho.
The wind—

I dusted small stones from my blood-knees. Spent
another year in fear, hiding and hexing

with Maria, my inner Italian witch (always female).
I didn't mean for him to die

in a Philly crackhouse. I didn't plan
for that. I just kept waiting for the pilot

to land the fucking plane. Take me away. So what.
So what he's dead.

The rain gutter deserves a better cleaning (1997)

At night my corduroy shorts
take the window frame with them,

a sweep of gray across one leg.

To sit & smoke on roof slats,
to watch the tea billow

from the curve of the tin can.

Here, the bird
had a way
of whistling less invasively.

It's time for dinner.

A friend taught me this.
You can use almost anything—

a cigarette, a Pepsi, an apple.

Down the aluminum stairs
to hear magnified a rattle of glass like plates

beneath a lawnmower.

Whose turn is it to say grace?

I never did learn the twist
of spaghetti in the cup of a spoon. To shovel

was so much easier.

Drug Buddy

ACT UP's Treatment and Data Team assigns
medications for members to study.

Take my hand, little Dextran Sulfate,
feel my palm clench. I'll take you

to my favorite place—it's this rooftop
that belongs to rich people whose doorman

never looks up from his paper. I brought nips
we can pour into your orange juice & pass

between our mouths. I'll tell you a little
about me, my parents I only see

once a year, the ones whose Reagan worship
I ran from. I'll tell you my lover's

triggers, like when I leave
the cabinets open, tell you

how we met (he was handing out
condoms). I'll tell you more, then quiet

down when the sun starts to sag a bit.
Then you tell me: they call this the *dyadic effect*,

you tell me about you. Dissolve. We're friends now.
I'll press you underneath my tongue. You can stay there

for years. I'll smoke your menthol cigarette
even though I quit. Our secret.

I'll tell you the bartender's name at the Pyramid,
the one with the softball shoulders who arches

his back when he bends over to crack
a Corona. I'll tell you his name

& that I almost slept with him.
I'll almost tell you I slept with him.

Maybe I'll save that for next time.
And you can tell me too. Tell me

what you'd do to the body.

Abecedarian in a Gay Porn

Again, his fingers clutch some phallic hope for spurts of jizz
blended with the sweat off his forehead, little pony
cantering away against a rocky bedframe. Relax.
Didn't we say this was only sex? He can paw
erratically at my chest all he wants. The Latin *viv*,
for life, as in vivacious, vitality, vivisection. Here in Xanadu,
gleaming with oils, I can pull his hair, eyes shut, limbs bent,
heaving breath (or is that the open window?) rising with the harness
I attached in the ringing of silver chains. If he can't grunt, he'll purr
just fine. Less gnarl, less curl, less tuft of opium, maybe, but still all tranq—
Kleptomania of the body, if you will. Keep surging till you pop
like a light bulb shining for fifty years, flicked off, then on again. O!
Mr. Edison & how now he rattles! Suck of grime, pluck of tin
nestled in my groin. He stays there, almost weeping like the sum
of all parts conceived to repeat their best factory moves. I call,
performative as it is, sucked in like a vacuum, this hard prick
queering my mouth like the fire sign he is. You know: Such a Sadj,
ready to bark at any sign of an east wind. Maybe it's just how I
slide my tongue up his neck then breathe. Arch his back. Now hush.
Truth: it's the core of a man I like best. A slim muscled stomach bang
unfurling from the navel. Bicycle crunch. Archaic torso. Scruff
varnishing its way into the circle around our cocks. Happy trails. May we
watch this again & again should we film it. Each unfolded release, each pound
Xanthus & Balius approved. Daddy Poseidon too. What a sauc-
y motherfucker, getting us all so close to the sea, only to stab
zest for the sake of watching the colors go, one more burst of flora.

Inventing Safe Sex: Questions between Richard Berkowitz & Michael Callen

Read this part again.
Was I too easy on the saliva? Too hard

on the urine? Is there enough
preambling here? Enough

context? What's our stance on anal?
Do we sound too traditional? We haven't even

mentioned lube. Who will help us
edit this & who

are we going to have print it?
How many? Five thousand. Too much?

Can we even afford that?
We haven't even mentioned love.

Who can we ask for the money?
Where should we hand it out?

Right, the Bar on Second Avenue.
The Pyramid.

And the World on Second.
We haven't even mentioned love.

Should we charge anything?
Read this part again.

Too condescending? Too preachy?

Too pompous too soapbox too pulpit?
How do we touch him

without dying?
Read this part again.

Beautiful People

after David Wojnarowicz

Wake to weight in the grip of your mug & drink
before you scrub your face with foam to shave
a razor down the skin—the eyelid brush, pink

around the hollows of your eyes, make up left to sink
down the center of your cheek bones, a church's nave.
Awake to a weight in the grip of your mug, drink

just a sip. & before panty hose rises above the hair of your waist, wink
at your black wig, your pearls, your dolls & mirror's shockwave.
A razor down the skin, now the eyelid brush—pink

to match your pearls, your dress, those dolls in a toolbox, you think:
run away change my name. Maria. Hail the cab, heels to the pave-
ment, what I meant: Wake to the weight of your mug, drink,

set it down, bob your wig with a cabbie over a bridge's kinks—
Cross Bronx to GW, out to the sounds of gulls who burst from graves
like a razor up the skin, smooth for the eyelid brush of pink

& now the holy forest, the rocks & flowers of zinc,
all around me black & white shifts to flush of flesh, red dress: a cave
wakened by the weight in the grip of your ABBA mug. Now drink

the lake water. Listen: Hum of electric wires while the rest think
high time that you found out frogs & crickets sound like they're drowning. Save
the razor that went down the skin, smoothed for the eyelid brush of pink.

Into the lake, into the crickets, into the owl hoots submerged in your sink
run away change my name become a woman forget the whole grave.
Wake to weight in the grip of your drink
a razor down the skin, lifting the eyelids, brushed pink.

Rubin

August 2006

In you, an east facing window

In you, the free condom I won't use

In you, a man hard & shirtless in a garden

behind Spiritus Pizza in you

a slow tide crawls into salt marsh

In you, the day I panic the day I ask

How do you even contract it?

In you extended release capsules, cell counts, IV tubes

In you I am I am

low risk or high risk I can't remember

In you years & years

In you my name you won't remember

In you my opportunistic infection

In you disease as metaphor

In you the apple

In you the sleep of apples

In you I am not are you

iii. we stuck our hard dicks in

He bitterly complained that the community that inherited the advances he helped wrought, who lived integrated lives as gay citizens . . . had abandoned his generation and forgotten the events that had shaped them.
—David France

Reverse Abecedarian with Missing Vowels

Zydeco chest beats break around
your shadows, tap each one on the
X-ray & ask what it is or where it came from or
who—a distant orb dancing across the city, his
vestiges dropping to the ancient carpet.
Take, for example, a heart valve, slow pump of
static blood, then blow yourself into it, swim,
raise both drum sticks & bang each one against this
quiet. The neighbors poke their brooms through the ceilings,
pause & listen to the beat through a pint glass.
Near the doors of the hospital, do you turn to a
man you met & say:
Let's not know? Or *Is it safe?*
Knowing each other? That well? That
J you carved into the willow tree: What did that stand for?
How did you even get the switchblade into the arboretum?
Grimace away the chatter of those entering be-
fore you—each bird sings its mating song louder the next day,
deteriorates its vocal cords against its wide breath until
crows, the whole murder of them, enter the willow, one by one,
before you.

Notes for a concrete poem

i.

The gray matted wall / to wall carpeting leads to this board / room again. Follow until you hit / a stench of oak, / now stench of cherry. Whiff of a rose. Dying / hydrangea. Centered sunflower. Chirp / of a brown leather chair wheeling across the weakening / floor boards. Stacks of papers rustle across the cold table. / See? See this number clawing at the mountain? / Squint past the blurs. If you can't focus, / then it's the distraction: porcelain vase / on the center of the table— / all the primary colors of a floral bouquet / rubbing together like the men at the Pyramid. / With this earthquake, how could we even / expect it not to wobble in such low moans? / How could we expect the radius / not to lengthen the way it does on the rolled skin / of a dollar bill? To now topple? / No one even reaches / for a towel. All the research soaks it up / in scatterplots with ink fading / like watercolor. Dehydrated stems. If we leave / it there, it takes the finish / right off.

ii.

"I had drawing that night. And, instead of going to drawing, I went to ACT UP. And I actually never went back to drawing."—Mark Harrington

Jericho

for Peter Staley
Offices of the FDA, 1988, Rockville, MD

Swell the street the concrete
        the wherewithal dirt stain it in your
                once worn high tops drag the left

the right across the pavement pass
        each fallen corpse laid across
                New Hampshire Avenue penny-eyed or

dead-gazed in arrows to the moving clouds stop
        to erect the lemonade stand
                pedal the pills keep walking

& when you get there *seize control*
        with a linked arm latching like
                hundreds of locked steel triangles

little percussive wands banging into
        pitched slow decay of sound
                then look up. It's Peter. He's rising

in bombs of smoke, black jeans planted
        like incensed trees
                rooted on the portico

hands stuffed in his bomber
        black jacket head up & banner
                behind, one cresting shroud.

Rag Protest, 1985

One of the first documented direct actions for AIDS activism was against the New York Post *and its columnist, Ray Kerrison.*

You in that shiny brown suit yeah you rag
along with your wall words
this rag bombs down raining
rags torn fisted rags

cotton rag old sheet rag bundled
rag to stuff in your ragwort mouth
down that ragweed throat a whipped rag
a twisted cracked thrown Rag-

gedy Ann. Andy. You
rag muffin you old rag
raggin on us in your ragtime
geezer raggedy suit? Here—

take the dust, the restaurant oil,
the school board floor soil, the chalk dust
take all we've wiped I hear
you can get it from sweat

Pyramid

Follow until you hit the stench of oak, now stench of cherry wood.

Whiff of a rose. Dying hydrangea. Sunflower. A chirp of a brown leather chair wheeling across the floor boards. Instead of going to drawing.

Stacks of papers rustle across the table. See? See this number clawing at the mountain? I see.

Do you see? Squint past

the burst? If you can't focus,

then it's the porcelain vase, center of the table

How could we

expect the radius

not to widen?

all the primary colors in the bouquet

of flora. With this earthquake

how could we even expect it not to wobble?

In such low moans?

To topple over now? No one reaches for a towel.

The gray matter wall-to-wall carpeting leads into a board room again.

All the research soaks it up in the scatterplots with ink fading like watercolor. Dehydrated stems. If we leave there, it takes

the finish right off.

I went to ACT UP.

Wellcome

Burroughs Wellcome Offices, Research Triangle Park, NC. April 25, 1989

You park a rusting
car at the offices
facing this highway
& walk, chest

out, into a fume
a future, some space
ship cloaked as office.
To ask the guard

directions is to learn
a way, learn how
those wing
tips clock

against the tile—how
the doors open on your bee-
line to the elevator.
How we rise.

*

I am holding
        a Teenage
                Mutant Ninja Turtle

named Rafael, and when
        I set him on the scratch
                of an indigo wall-

to-wall carpet, my sister
        sets a tube
                of lipstick

on my mouth,
        tucks barrettes
                in my hair, names me:

Maria.

*

You say, *Ma'am, there's a situation on this floor. Calmly*
          proceed to the lobby & when the rest
follow, do you enter an office

at random? Do you call Steve & Jay
          sitting on a hotel bed, toes tapping
a salmon carpet, bodies rocking

in the dim light?   Do you lock the door?

*

A cartographer maps
          dystopia, its tiny pyramids
                    of office buildings sketched

of eighties brutalism. Or is this futurism?

*

The daffodil
and the little girl,
my sister sings

& I open
my ruby mouth.
Daffodil. Short A.

*

A bus   to North Carolina. The Heart
of Durham Hotel   thirty-seven a night.

A shared bed   a wrestle with a floral
comforter in a   one-eyed sleep.   Awake

to the cymbals of a wake-   up call:

*

Anointed: *Maria*. We pick daffodils.
        One, I hold to my face for a close-up.
                Yellow sun ablaze in light

        red lipstick, red sash
                around Rafael's eyes,
                        nearly blindfolded.

*

With erased earrings, you press
        a suit with a hotel iron, cloak
your tattoos, & tuck names beneath

a wool-blended blazer—Jay, Deb, Steve, & Dan,
        Executive drag. Lee, Blane, James, & Peter.
Comb the tussles of your damp hair & place

the sandwiches, the water, the heart,
        in all its veins & brass beatings,
in the fake leather folds of your brief case.

*

Release the knob & barricade. *I am holding*
wait for the sirens. Pour your breath
through the receiver & tell the others *nearly*
blindfolded to send the press release. *We are not*
leaving. When the police arrive, your script:

We are nonviolent, unarmed, & we are not leaving
until & once the walls the walls begin to shake,
until Burroughs Wellcome agrees to lower
your own handcuffs *barrettes in my hair.* Now
here's your back against the heat *agrees to lower*

pull out the chain, the lock & cuff *a Teenage*
Mutant Ninja from the sweating pleather
of a brief case *agrees to lower the price of AZT*
& chain yourself to the radiator.

Wellcome Detail

Prior to taking over the pharmaceutical company, Burroughs Wellcome, in 1988, ACT UP activists booked the Heart of Durham Hotel.

heart of durham a twenty a ten a five & two ones donated
by someone with a twenty a ten a five & two ones
handed to a mustached clerk at a large oak desk
to share two beds to share the heart
of durham hotel room   room with a balcony
what comfort a blue room with
whiff of old comforter shaken not washed
threads fraying in the april breezy heart
of durham room with color
tv a balcony next to
a room with a balcony & a rotary phone
that dings when you move it
room with a comforter pulled upon
two beds   room with a vacuumed
carpet with a little couch that maybe doesn't pull out
open the balcony doors wider heart
of durham   a dim yellow lamp lit into
blue walls   a press room   a rotary phone singing
a release pressing into a key clack in the heart
of durham hotel   feed the paper into its dial
press down each key pound   feed
the paper   a yellow
bathroom even soap we can use to dress up
we are executives we are professionals we are
briefcases ties starch & wingtips
even a pool no one will swim in
because it is cold & april

but this is *our* pool we have a key
is this a tenement   no it is the heart of durham hotel
who pays the cashier who takes the key who
the couch doesn't pull out who cares
who shares each bed with cum stains
with a grumpy ice machine & plumbing that leaks
with a rotary phone that dings
when you move it

Wall Street

New York Stock Exchange, September 1989

Money green money float
money rock money back
into air forth green sway
cradle hand over
balcony green wave
over wave overhead eyes
large & green fixed over
head money up money down *money*
it's a gas breathe in money pushed
by vents green money paper thin
buoy money now rise into air push
money out to ride the vent thin
green arcs like *dollar dollar*
bill y'all thousands of green
crescent moon dance money
the money swing of pendulum
always sunny eyes wide
in a rich man's world with
green saliva fling of wrist
wraith money *I make it rain*
money the green raindrops mouth
open feed the spleen money *the best*
things in life are free but you
can give them money up swarm
of money look at all that *all*
about the benjamins money
floating green birds from

this spit money machine look
up money look down into
cloud viridian look money
behind money this crawling
fog like bees go
snatch it.

Coalescence

for Steven Cordova

1.

What were they going to do to us? Run over us?
Because this action   was Supreme
because they had dragged   each other
across concrete in preparation
Because Gaëton because   Jeffrey because

the tight plastic handcuffs

Kneel.   A fed with a camera.

2.

Because   in a basement garage,

their rented bus parks
& because the busses of the other

groups caravan behind & because, just minutes before,
they were pinching the window
levers & snapping

up panes in a song of unison,
just minutes before saying
I can't wait to pee &

How much longer?

& because up the windows went,
with an exhale from the long 95 South highlight
(New York to DC),

they open the door to squint: the white
light shoots like cannons from motorcycles
encircled in grind & pitched revs

3.

I don't kneel.

&, despite all the practice *the only person*
resisting
the cops not dealing with me well
a tensed muscle thrashes the grip
my affinity group really coalesced around me
body forward body backward

to make sure that I was okay
& now a click notches the pinch of plastic cuffs
& now a large glass elevator ascends through

a federal prison.   Now it passes
five Black men in a chain gang
& this, the Supreme Court—

& this wrist singed. & this one.
& this again—

Bowers vs. Hardwick

We bent the horse over & stuck our hard dicks in
We bent the lamp over & stuck our hard dicks in
We bent the rocking chair over, couldn't find a hole,
unplugged a peg & stuck our hard dicks in
We told the dog come here & stuck our hard dicks in
We took the floppy discs out of DOS computers
& stuck our hard dicks in
We took down all the art in the MET, neatly,
packaged it away, then in the empty frames,
we stuck our hard dicks in
We found a vacuum at a garage sale by St. Peter's, plugged it in,
then turned it over & stuck our hard dicks in
We popped out the *Mario Bros. 3* cartridge, & into the Nintendo,
we stuck our hard dicks in
We opened every washer door at the Laundromat on 7th
& stuck our hard dicks in   We pressed
on   The water swirled around & around & it felt good
We ordered beers at the bar & when they wouldn't serve us
we took their empty pint glasses & stuck our hard dicks in

We told the horse to neigh louder   the dog to bark like a dog
We searched for each other's mothers
We searched for each other's fathers & grandfathers
We went to graveyards, dug up old caskets, rattled decaying bones,
We went to parks
full of trees with knotted trunks
& holes holes holes

Squirrels scratched & we bled
We found a lighthouse by each of the five oceans,
turned on all the lights so that
finally, after we had climbed down those spiral staircases
to reach one another, to stare into the deep moonlit roses
of each other's eyes, each pupil blinking against all that circling
white light,
we had gone
soft

iv. mirror for mirror

And when it became time to go
they none of them would leave without the other
—John Ashbery

Stoke

My lover and I didn't bring enough kindling
to ignite the night's beach fire. It's November,
we're cold, & everyone knows Vaseline is flammable.

Just along the dune's barrier, I clasp a piece of driftwood,
large, splintery log carried back for the sacrifice—
when, together, we heave out our breaths, the whole of it

up in flames, our lungs such thin red balloons. One at a time
we rip pages from Leviticus, just to keep it roaring. Embers rise
like ivy stretching for the moon. Each time a page burns

its cold alphabet, our heads jerk to the sound of
a smashed window. Each time we return
our gaze to each other, we search for beach glass

in each other's eyes, four windows, our almost mirrors
of soft orange no, soft yellow. Scratch that:
I call it color, but really, isn't it just that? Light.

Variations on a Theme in Blue

after Derek Jarman

~~The film~~ ***Blue* is meant to be** ~~viewed on a large screen & I know this, but once captured by the blue screen of my phone I decide to substitute my phone's screen with~~ **the blue around me.** ~~Listen to the audio only; stare at something blue. Jarman's sight deteriorated during the production of this film, which, against a large blue rectangle, is~~ **an assemblage of sounds moving in and out of** ~~Jarman's life in 1992 as a man with retinitis caused by HIV. Here, at the library, I leave the phone on my lap & stare at the carpet and the book shelves, both blue, but lighter shades than~~ **the cyan across the long** ~~rectangle~~ **drape**~~d across my lap. The color, of course, depends on the~~ **light**~~. When one~~ **looks for** ~~various websites from which to obtain the film, a collage of~~ **thumbnails** ~~appears on the bootlegged versions, all blue rectangles, all the same blue family: *David Howard Graham Terry Paul*~~

~~Sound of a gong.~~ **Harps** ~~pluck a blue chord, while instructions *Look down look left look right the camera flash*~~ **weave into** ~~the Provincetown Library, next to a life size ship, a model of the *Rose Dorthea*. I look out a window & watch a ray of sun beckon.~~

~~I pause the film & walk to~~ **the beach where** ~~I lie across a towel striped in~~ **two shades of light and dark blue**~~. Lying with my head on a backpack, I stare at a cloudless sky while I~~ **listen.**

~~YouTube plays a commercial. Shoes. Buy shoes. Jarman's film is not meant for a beach, for a sky, or commercials, and now I feel guilty, as though I'm stealing something or cheating.~~ **I should have** ~~planned better, should have put the headphones on at a library monitor, borrowed a projector, found myself a quiet, dark space. I pause everything to swim. Bayside Provincetown at~~ **high tide, deep enough.** ~~Past~~ **rocks**~~, grain, and sand, I wade and dunk,~~ **kick through the soft denim surf.** ~~Once ready to rejoin Jarman's *Blue*, the index toe on my left foot stings. When I look down, it's bleeding.~~ **A broken shell.**

~~Back into the tide to wash it,~~ **the blood from** ~~the toe's ball leaks from its curved slit into~~ **the ocean**~~, a bright red melding into deep blue. When it surfaces it still~~ **bleeds. Clean.** ~~The ocean blue meets a blue sky and look. Look how the shades are lighter the closer they are to earth.~~

~~"~~**Time is what** ~~keeps the light from reaching us," Jarman says when~~ **I return to** ~~*Blue*. Boat sails cut into~~ **the horizon**~~. An orange kayak~~ **passes.** ~~A buoy's blue stripe wraps around its waist.~~ **Horns.** ~~An electric guitar. A later high tide~~ **today, at five**~~, and now Jarman asks, "What do they pay~~ **the ferryman**~~?" When the toe surfaces it~~ **still bleeds.** ~~I guess I could call it clean.~~

A Rose for Simon

a golden shovel after phrases from Mark Doty's "Demolition"

Remember how we polished rocks with our upside-down bike wheels? We
remember, or try to, our fingernails clawed in dirt to pluck the hard clay, pull love.
Remember the cushions we'd pounce to avoid lava? Such upholstered disasters.
Remember that those cushions saved us only briefly in there, in that?
Remember to hold, to have.
Remember nothing.
Remember how we'd play that light-up game? Simon? How we'd have to
remember each hot bright rectangle—red, yellow, green, blue—to un-do.
Remember we'd pound every square we could fight with?
Remember this game of memory as us.
Remember that we, together, could have been joined.
Remember the sea salt we ate by the oceans we sat by.
Remember to press a lit square, a red, a blue, a green, a—
Remember? I forget. Such aggressive buzzing. Such thirst.
Remember all the sirens we'd watch out for?
Remember Pedro, from *The Real Word*, our blooming eyes watching?
Remember anything, remember something.
Remember the way, from the bikes we'd fall:
Remember how we'd get up, limping, unmuted & teary, unable.
Remember to connect this memory to the collective disappearing memory, to
remember what everyone wants to forget.
Remember the way we spelled each word, our affix analysis, the
remember being broken into re-, into member, into my mirror's vain.
Remember they were dying while you were playing memory games &
remember that if you think they didn't carve you this space, then you're stupid.
Remember, boy.
Remember them, her, his, him, he.

Remember how their bodies on the pavement allowed—
Remember how *their* bodies on the pavement allowed you to
remember ruin,
remember him.

Abecedarians with Consonants Who Have Left First the Party and Then Their Bodies

All this time, you thought the driftwood
expanded with the heat of a beach fire?
I told you it would it soon be ash, an ember
of our existence as we threw a Frisbee
under each other's legs on a beach on Fire Island.
You lost it in the dunes. Now go find it.

*

Away from the key rattle of an office,
exiled from a bathroom, a school, a hospital
into you I return like the scratch on a vinyl,
our favorite song, little Freddie, little Bowie,
under the pressure of a kiln melting glass blown:
You are blown & that is safer.

*

Acquiescence to these stigmata keeps blood pouring
endlessly into a carafe set in the center of a table
I set a leaf into yesterday. Today is the party. Today we
offer a chalice spilling its crimson into the air
under a chandelier that his fingers keep dimming
yes dimming as I strain to make this toast into your eyes

*

& you raising yours too, the way a ghost leaves its body
extended just above the chest—&
isn't that just it? The rising, I mean. The way it moves
out & then in. But more out. Then
under
you.

Command

It's nearing Easter. My lover, David, & I watch *The Ten Commandments* with Charlton Heston. We break it up across three days, one hour per day. I always associated Heston with the NRA, with white old man gun-toting *uhmerca* toxic masculinity, but the more I watch, the more Moses's shoulders & thighs seem to flex, seem to bulge out of the screen, oiled.

In this narrative, Moses seems, quite naturally, gay to me—stoic, slightly neurotic in his ethics, & completely unchanged by every advance from a smoking-hot Nefretiri. Part of me wants them to fuck just so I can see the balls of his bare arms, the sweat on his chest, his sleepy bedroom eyes. The other part of me wants him to get it on with Joshua, muscled by Pharaoh's hard labor, bronzed by an Egyptian sun, &, also a babe.

In my version, there is no risk: Moses parts the Red Sea. But he doesn't marry the shepherd's daughter. After the bush burns, he brings Joshua up to the mountain to show him where God spoke. Joshua looks him in the eye, takes his hand, & before either of them can even think it, pulls him toward his mouth.

Memorial

after Laura Ewing's sculpture

& how did this black ocean wash up here? Onyx carbon quartzite, airlifted onto
the town lawn, a sandstone metamorphose into two affixed forms,
& whose etches?
In what font? Is this just one tidal black moment, or a collection of them
as in, one wave cannot be one atom, one molecule, compound
one wind, one wave but a
Isn't a wave just a magnet for the moon, the earth a spin
then curl from the morning moisture? & take, for example, the ocean:
the way our spines suffer
How do you make a cast of it? & then, a mold?
of gray, here, now, what we call a mark & aren't those quick flecks
of survival? It says, *Remembering.*
The waves, though dark, blind: not one
Repeat it.
but a gathering of them, so that
if we can, at best, preserve these forms, can we also cup their hands?
Can we, at least,
the wave?

Parallel Trial

To allow expediated availability of drugs for people living with HIV, Jim Eigo, an ACT UP activist, negotiated the first instance of "compassionate use" with the FDA in 1988.

When all the lines of a broken brown building
        & all the bricks so heavy with neglect,
each heavy glass door another entry to another door

        & another door after that (this one's blue)
& all the whiffs of an underfunded public school
        all the steps to lift my calves

all the unfiltered air at the top of the stairs
        lead to another door to walk through (this one's red).
Now in the board room, the long table.

        Now in the board room, Rockville light
which bleaches all of us.
        Now in the board room, a chair with lumbar support

& now the chair muffles against an abused carpet.
        Now in the board room so many oversized blazers
& lab coats interrupted from labs in the board room

        so many heterosexual Windsor knots
& pleats.
        In the board room fluorescent lights rocking my legal

pad back & forth like someone who knows how to talk & is talking.
        In the board room my yellow lined paper
my notes from Iris

        my lungs my breath of stale fluorescent air
& my voice like dead ivy
        come back to life, a tear

in the leaf, a stretch in stomata
        a growth in the bud, an opening vein
wave of stipule, each living frond, a word negotiated.

I pull it crawling from my throat
        in the board room.
Ivy all over the long table.

Last Supper

Dear David France, Dear Peter Staley,
Dear Steven, Sara, Sonia, D. A., Essex, & Paul,
Dear Matthew, Mark, Luke. Dear John,

At this, your maple table, you ask me to pull
the ends out.
Set the leaf in. Push harder
so the ends set.

You lay the purple
tablecloth. Move the bird, little centerpiece,
roll out a blueprint. All the starched vestments—

At grace, a man says, *I am grateful for your wide eyes, the tear*
ducts that saved them,
each corneal mirrored registration.

You point to your eyes, say *I am grateful for these crow's feet,*
for the flecks of ash gray
in each eyebrow.

I am grateful, I say, *that you hit*
reply, that you lived
to tell it right. Dear David,

dear Alan, dear Sara, dear Jay & Carl, dear Richard Berkowitz
& Michaels Callen & Cunningham, Marks Doty & Harrington, dear Love,

birds take on the language of their feathers. Brave pollinators.

You rise from the table head,
                                        pick from your garden
                                the largest rose

& pass it.
        Here it is, bloodshot flora, plated for the banquet.

I pick each petal
                        place it in my mouth,
then let this tongue burn a flame blue.

On Saving the Old Bouquet

Lately, a child whose heart is so full
they arrive to school opening their mouth
& spilling from their lips the whole floral section
of Stop n Shop. We cup the flowers in our hands
& shirts. I help dust the petals.
Each rose is a memory flaking.

Lately, an adult who looks at the time on his phone
then uses its light to walk by. His footsteps are ticking,
his heels kick up hourglass sand. He looks back
& back & back again, as though searching
for Lot's wife, his mother, forever Sodom's salt.

Lately, we blow into our mugs. It is wine, but no one
deserves to know this. Pinot. Me & you.
I use Scotch tape to hang tea strings from the lips
of our vessels. They dangle like two sunrises.

Lately, the sun stays hanging in the air & guilting us all into play.
Lately, I play. The rules are broken, the sun rays
disenthralled. If I miss the dead too much,
they follow me into my dreams, pulling out chairs
in their kitchens. Over coffee, over tea,

they sing, *Spill! Spill the petals all over your precious tile floors!*
They harmonize like Simon & Garfunkel.
They flop through pages & pages of their diaries.
They open a window & let the pollen in.

notes

"Rare Cancer" borrows language from "Pneumocystis Pneumonia—Los Angeles," *MMWR Weekly* (June 5, 1981), and from Lawrence K. Altman, "Rare Cancer Seen in 41 Homosexuals," *NY Times* (1981), two of the first major articles written about AIDS.

"Elegy for Gaëton Dugas" borrows quotes directly from news headlines, from Randy Shilts, and from a former publicist at St. Martin's Press for Shilts' text, *And The Band Played On: Politics People and the AIDS Epidemic.*

"Billboard of an empty bed" is after the public artwork by Félix González-Torres of the same title.

"Inventing Safe Sex: Questions between Richard Berkowitz & Michael Callen" references the composition of the pamphlet *How to Have Sex in an Epidemic: One Approach.*

"Godspell" is for Jeffrey Mylett, June 8, 1949–May 7, 1986.

"Lung Study" addresses the role of citizen-led science in the battle for AIDS research.

The title of section ii ("the coat room was the first to go") refers to the Stonewall Riots of 1969 in which the bar's coat closet was the first thing to be set on fire. The commentary from Sonia Sanchez reflects on her family's experience with her brother who died from AIDS-related complications.

"Neighbors" refers to the Delaware County, Pennsylvania, nightclub Pulsations, which hosted a robot, 10 dance floors, and 11 bars. It closed in 1994.

"Wind in the Air, Wind in the Lungs" is for a former student, J. W. The poem also references Italian American witchcraft, as documented in "Imagining the Strega: Folklore Reclamation and the Construction of Italian American Witchcraft" by Sabina Magliocco.

Italicized lines in "I, Barbie" are taken from Paul Lisicky's *Later: My Life at the Edge of the World.*

"Drug Buddy" is for Mark Harrington. In the ACT UP Oral History Project, Mark, a member of the Treatment and Data Team of ACT UP, in discussing his role in drug research, states, "We had drug buddies. So, once we had a list of stuff that we thought was interesting, we would assign a member . . . to sort of become that drug's buddy." In the same interview, Schulman asks Harrington where he would go for fun, to which Harrington replies, "The Pyramid, the World. Remember the World?"

"Beautiful People" is after David Wojnarowicz's film of the same title.

In "Rubin," the line "the sleep of apples" references Federico García Lorca's poem "Gacela of the Dark Death."

"Jericho" is for Peter Staley, whose direct actions, including climbing the canopy of the FDA building, are documented in his memoir, *Never Silent.*

"Rag Protest" refers to the protest against the *New York Post*'s columnist Ray Kerrison, who early on propagated myths that gay men brought AIDS on themselves. The protest against the *Post* is one of the first documented direct actions taken by a group of people surrounding the AIDS crisis.

Names in "Wellcome" refer to Jay Blotcher, Peter Staley, Steve Rosenbush, Deb Gavito, Blane Mosely, Lee Arsenault, James McGrath, and Dan Baker.

"Wall Street" borrows from the songs of Pink Floyd, Wu Tang Clan, Barrett Strong, ABBA, and Fat Joe featuring Lil Wayne.

"Variations on a Theme in *Blue*" is after Derek Jarman's film.

"Parallel Trial" is for Jim Eigo, who negotiated the first compassionate use drug trials with the FDA, effectively saving countless lives.

"Memorial" is based on Lauren Ewing's memorial located on the town lawn of Provincetown, MA.

Thank you to Ted Kerr and Alexandra Juhasz, whose work allowed me to better understand the cultural production across HIV status, race, age, gender, and socioeconomic status. As a white, queer, HIV negative body, I approach this work as an homage to those that have allowed me this privilege.

All poems are informed by *Let the Record Show* by Sarah Schulman, *How to Survive a Plague: The Inside Story of How Citizens and Science Tamed AIDS* by David France, the ACT UP Oral History Project, Instagram's AIDS Memorial, and personal interviews with survivors of the epidemic.

acknowledgments

Grateful acknowledgement is given to the editors and staff of the following journals who first published some of these poems or their earlier iterations:

& Change: "Wall Street" and "Notes for a Concrete Poem"; *Black Warrior Review*: "Coalescence"; *B O D Y*: "Abecedarians with Missing Consonants"; Broadsided Press published "Collective Memory" as a broadside (titled "Obituary"); *The Bubbler*: "Rubin"; *Cincinnati Review*: "35-Year-Old Man Shares Joint Near Harbor of Gay Resort Town"; *Crab Creek Review*: "Wellcome Detail"; *Cream City Review*: "Bowers vs. Harwick" and "Abecedarian with Missing Vowels [Broken from the one step]"; *Foglifter*: "Parallel Trial" and "Reverse Abecedarian with Missing Vowels"; *Free State Review*: "Wind in the Air, Wind in the Lungs"; *Frozen Sea*: "Boy in a Turban Holding a Nosegay"; *Gulf Coast*: "Window"; *J Journal*: "Rag Protest, 1985"; *Juked*: "Elegy for Gaëton Dugas"; *Michigan Quarterly Review*: "Rare Cancer"; *Ocean State Review*: "Neighbors"; *Prairie Schooner*: "Death of the Sperm Whale" (titled "Lagoda"); *Provincetown Independent*: reprint of "Elegy for Gaëton Dugas"; *River Teeth*: "Command"; *Southern Indiana Review*: "Variations on a Theme in Blue"; *Variant Lit*: "On Saving the Old Bouquet"; *Verse Daily*: "The rain gutter deserves a better cleaning."

whether or not we knew them we are saying thank you
—W. S. Merwin

Outside of the Ancestors, historians, and activists who became this book, I am sloppily spilling my gratitude on everyone's party dresses, especially those that lent their time to provide feedback on earlier versions of this manuscript—Eve Alexandra, Kazim Ali, Martha Collins, Lee Herrick, Laura McCullough, Patricia Smith, and Brian Turner.

My perpetual thanks to Honorée Fanonne Jeffers, who chose this work for the Donald Hall Prize. You are the truth-to-power I had hoped would see my work and the fact that it resonated with you carries with it my deepest pride. And to those initial readers that put it in her hands—you are both nameless and gorgeous.

My Cape Cod writing community, the Bass River Revisionists, read many early versions of these poems and provided thoughtful hawk-eyes, feedback, and love: Susan Berlin, Deirde Callanan, Robin Clarke, Betty Ann Lauria, Mary Ellen Redmond, Carole Stasiowski, and Lauren Wolk. Community torch-bearers Joe Gouveia, Greg Hischak, and John Landry taught me the power of the mic which became the power of the body which also became many of these poems.

Tina Pellegrino and Boyd Jorden, my early teachers, handed me flint for the fire. Countless educators afterward offered patience, guidance, and encouragement to continue the trudge: Laure Anne Bossellaar, Garrard Conley, Nick Flynn, Chris Hosea, John Murillo, Ronaldo Wilson, and Mark Wunderlich. The Fine Arts Work Center in Provincetown provided invaluable support in the form of scholarships whereby I could learn from this army.

Ed and Betty, my first teachers, my parents, cloaked me in love—which is resilience—and then doubled-down on that by instilling values in education, which is how we critique systems and take back our power; my sisters, Chrissie and Beth Ann, gave me my inner *Maria* and handed me that daffodil, while my brother, Brian, guided me into the laughter, independence, cigarettes, and ponchos of a necessary, quieter masculinity (I'm sure there's still some Camel Light butts in that rain gutter). To my other fountains of courage: Gemma Leghorn, Anne Needel, the Rivera family, and so many former students.

To David, for David, and for handing me those condoms on the fourth of July. Your heart is contagious. You are beautiful, and I am sorry my phone is always on silent.

And for everyone who's acting up and fighting back right now—breathe in your lineage. Expand your chest with it. We built this; it's ours. We take it back.